A WELDER'S GUIDE TO HANDRAILS

And Railing Codes

BY
KY BENFORD

Copyright © 2022 by Ky Benford

All rights reserved. This book or any portion thereof may not be reproduced or used in any manner whatsoever without the express written permission of the publisher except for the use of brief quotation in a book review.

ISBN 979-8-9857416-3-6

Table of Contents

Introduction 1
Fabrication Tools 3
Installation Tools 5
How We Got Here 6
Q & A 8
Terminology 9
Before We Get Into The Minutiae of the Code 11
Appendix 13
References 22

Introduction

The world of welding can lead you down so many avenues. If you think about the different types of welders and their specialties, it's pretty extensive the lanes one could choose. You can practice in the field of general practice as a combination welder, or you could specialize in something like handrails. If you are reading these words you have probably crossed paths with the lane of handrails.

After being introduced to this entirely new world for me, I was immediately forced to scramble to find answers to the questions that each project introduced. However, I could not find clear direct answers to the questions in one place.

My name is Ky Benford, I am the owner of KBG Welding in Austin, Texas. Why did I write this book you ask? I wrote it because I am zealous about my faith in Christ and helping grow the welding community. The challenges you face if you are starting your own business are grand enough without having to worry about figuring out how to pass code with a handrail build.

What you will find in these pages are not only the answers, but a break-down of the terminology used in the code books and construction fields. I will also be sharing some of my personal experiences and guffaws that hopefully will keep you from repeating.

* The tools you will need to succeed
* The terminology
* The codes provided by the international standards
* Real life experiences

What you will need to succeed in this field and welding in general is the "Figure It Out" Factor. You will continually run into situations that will not have a clear cut or written answer. When you are in a stare down with one of these you will have to assess, ponder the options, pick the avenue you will take, and GO! You will quickly find that the longer you take getting to go, the more the project will drag out. And ultimately the project needs to be completed before you get paid. As you grow in experience, and trial and error, you will be better equipped to face troubling situations.

A friend of mine is a master mechanic. I used to stop by and visit him at his shop often, usually because I needed his services and I am not mechanically inclined. At his work station is a huge Snap-on tool box filled with a ton of tools for his trade. We would get on the topic of the cost of the tool box and how much he would spend on tools. To me the numbers were ridiculous. The other thing that perplexed me was that the Snap-on truck showed up every Friday and most of those stops included a new tool purchase. When I asked him why he said, "A mechanic is only as good as his tools." Tools make life easier. If you have the correct tools the tasks are less strenuous. This is true for the mechanic, dentist, and welder. If you have the correct tools you can kill it.

Fabrication Tools

1. Tape measure. Basic, but totally necessary. Knowing how to use it or read it doesn't hurt either. If you are struggling with reading a tape measure, or don't know how to use it at all, check out our KBG Welding YouTube channel video.

   https://www.youtube.com/shorts/bbQs4WuHpw0

2. Angle Finder or Bevel Gauge. This will help you find the angles and transfer them to the desired build. https://youtu.be/pVeOe0dBj1s

3. Speed Square. You can determine the angle a cut is or needs to be and you will need to have everything square, level, straight, plumb, or flush when building anything. (I will discuss this in an upcoming publication.)

4. Soap Stone. You may prefer silver streak or a Sharpie. With the proper use of a soap stone, you can get the precision of you marking down to about 1/32". If you use a Sharpie, you are looking at about 1/8" mark. The other downfall to using a Sharpie is that the marker will bleed through primer. https://youtu.be/REQI8cZi-4w

5. Grinder. You can use a 41/2" or 6" grinder. Dewalt, Milwaukee, Mutabo or Ridgid. I suggest that you use flap discs as opposed to hard discs. In this application you will beveling the joints before the weld and

grinding away the afterwards for a better aesthetic. In my opinion, hard discs are louder but not faster at grinding and leave a horrible finish. Flap discs do great. Make sure you bevel.

https://youtu.be/ZnGCAzWptTw

6. Squeeze Clamps. You will need some with pads to make sure they are flush and to hold them together in the fabrication process.

7. Picket Master Pro. This spacing tool eliminates time from the process of the build. No more calculating to find the proper spacing. Just lay this tool out and you will locate where each picket should go. https://www.saltcitysteel.org/shop/p/12point

8. Hammer. You can always use a hammer. Do not use other tools to do a hammer's job.

9. Mig Welder. We generally use innershield wire to eliminate the cost of gas. There is no rule for or against this option. We use Miller 211 or Lincoln 155.

10. Chopsaw. You can use a grinder with a cut off wheel if you chose to. For precision, the chopsaw is more consistent and accurate at keeping cuts straight.

11. Drill press or drill.

Installation Tools

1. Levels. 2-3' levels. Torpedo levels will work, but for accuracy larger levels are suggested.//
2. Drill/driver. With wood screws or torx screws.
3. Note that things happen. Don't freak out if an install does not fit correctly. It may be as simple as grinding down some material. It's not finished until its fixed, so might as well spend more time finishing then complaining.

How We Got Here

In middle school I was introduced to shop class. I was curious about doing things but didn't know anyone that did them. When I started class I was intrigued and ready to learn. My best friend Darrell and I worked on our wood projects in class. These had to be complete in time for the Christmas break. My project was a horse head clock for my stepfather. During the Christmas break, Darrell and I had a plan to utilize his stepfather's shop and build some wood items and sell them. We sold some, but didn't go viral and had to return to school after the break. This experience wasn't one that prepared me for the construction world. We used templates and weren't required to measure things.

When I started welding school, I was also working for a manufacturing company. I was required to learn how to read a tap measure. I had learned previously and was able to wing it most of the time. At this point in my career, I had to take ownership of this skill.

The first welding job that I had was doing precision welding of small components for the semiconductor world. This consisted of 90% Tig welding with tolerances of .003"-.005". A few years into this, I was offered a 'DD&T' class that taught us the intricacies of dimensions and tolerances. I highly suggest you take a class on it.

I did get some experience with some moderate sized frames that prepared me for future jobs. Namely, the firewood racks that we build and sell. We also sell the blueprints for anyone interested in building your own firewood rack. https://kbgwelding.com/store/ols/products/4x4-firewood-rack-blueprints

Whether you're starting a welding business or already have one, you know that running a business can be a challenge. There are plenty of ups and downs.

I experienced challenging times early in this business. I prayed for provision and opportunities. Not long after that, I get a phone call from a friend. He said a friend of his needed some help at work. He needed a welder to help him out for a couple of weeks as a contractor. What happened next was only God. During this time, I was introduced to the world of handrails and staircases.

Q & A

In the specialty of handrails what is one thing you wish you knew when you started?

"I should have made better use of the geometry classes!"
-@SantosIronWorks

"Field measuring correctly is one of the most important aspects of getting a quality railing and fitment."
-@NexusFabrication

"How to upsell. How to treat each transaction like this is good sale, but it can be better."
-@All_seasons_iron_works

"Be prepared to lose a lo of money for about 1-2 years. Year 3 I broke even. Year 4 I made 50k. Year 5 I make 200k."
-@seattle_city_steel

Terminology

1. Code standards The code is the standardized requirement for all builds. This is the standard set by the International Code Council (ICC). All builds must be maintained to the code standards approved by the City when the building was built and in compliance with the International Property Maintenance Code. Please understand that the code is your friend. Just like following blueprints can protect you from liability, so will the code. Work the code.

2. Treads. These are the actual top of the stair steps. When in construction, these will be installed late in the project.

3. Risers. The vertical height on the back of the step.

4. Nose. The part of the tread that extends past the riser.

5. Handrail. A rail fixed to posts or a wall for people to hold on for support.

6. Guardrail. A rail that prevents people from falling off or being hit by something.

7. Grab bar. A single rail fixed to wall or guard rail for people to hold on for support.

8. Finished floor height. The overall height of the floor once the finished flooring is installed.

9. Tread height. When treads are not installed, you have to account for the thickness of the tread to ensure you have proper height on your railing.

10. Flight. A stairway (set of steps) between one floor, or landing, and the next.

11. Blocking. The use of short pieces of dimensional lumber in wood framed construction to brace longer members or to provide grounds for fixing.

12. Pitch. This refers to height over run. What this means, is a ratio of the height achieved, verses run, in a roof, a slope, or anything that has a gradient involved.

13. Slope. A surface of which one end or side is at a higher level than another; a rising or falling surface.

14. Newels. A newel, also called a central pole or support column, is the central supporting pillar of a staircase. It can also refer to an upright post that supports and/or ruminates the handrail of a stair banister.

15. Balusters. Short column used in a group to support a rail. Commonly found on the side of a stairway; a banister.

16. Flush. Where joints align to provide a continuous look of the railing.

17. Level. Where railing is aligned perpendicular to the ground.

Before We Get Into
The Minutiae of the Code

Not everyone can appreciate and respect a finished handrail like someone that has authored its story. Just like anything else, handrails can be taken for granted. They can be overlooked or it can be an afterthought. That is until one is needed. Then you have to pay the bill.

Handrails are required. Period.

I was introduced to the world of handrails when I got a call from a friend who had a friend that owned a stair company. He was in a pinch and needed a hand on getting some builds out. This was this guy's world. Steel railings and wood. He had the process down. Working in his shop I was given a master class on handrail building. He would provide a drawing with angles and dimensions. However, I was slow at the math and couldn't get it down. It wasn't until I got out of the umbrella of his projects that I realized how important the angles and dimensions were, and how they are not figured out with arithmetic.

Since this encounter with a stair and railing master, I have built about 100 handrails and over a dozen staircases. All these experiences have not been textbook perfect, partly because I didn't have a textbook to go by. That's why you are reading these words now. I wanted to develop a textbook where my fellow tradesman could go to get the answers they needed to get to the master level. I want to share this with you who is willing to invest in yourself and your future the priceless lessons I've learned over the years.

Like grade school, I want to provide an answer key for the things you will face and the questions you will ask.

Appendix

Code

Must be maintained to the code standards approved by the City when the building was built and in compliance with the International Property Maintenance Code and local amendments. The rails must be firmly fastened and capable of supporting normally imposed loads.

Sections 304, 305, 307 (IPMC)

See Permit Exemption Code Reference, BCM Section 6.4. See Common Life Safety Components Chart, BCM Section 6.5.

305.1.1 Unsafe conditions. The following conditions violate this code and are declared unsafe:

1. A structure or a component of a structure cannot perform as intended;

2. A wall or column is not anchored to support a floor or roof;

3. Structural members, including stairs, landings, decks, balconies, walking surfaces, handrails, and guardrails, cannot perform as intended;

4. Structural members, including stairs, landings, decks, balconies, walking surfaces, handrails, and guardrails, are not anchored to support use of the structural member; or

5. Any portion of the foundation system is not supported by footings, is not supported by adequate soil, has cracks or breaks, or is not adequately anchored.

Exception: If a person, using an approved method, establishes that the condition is safe, then the condition does not violate this code.

307.1 General. Handrails and guards shall be maintained in good repair and in accordance with the Building Code in effect at the time of construction.

307.2 Handrails and guards required. Every exterior and interior flight of stairs having more than four rises shall have a handrail on one side of the stair. Every open portion of a stair, landing, balcony, porch, deck, ramp, or other walking surface that is more than 30 inches above the floor or grade below shall have guards. Handrails shall not be less than 30 inches in height or more than 42 inches in height measured vertically above the nosing of the tread or above the finished floor of the landing or walking surfaces. Guards, if required at the time of construction, shall be not less than 30 inches in height above the floor of the landing, balcony, porch, deck, ramp, or other walking surface.

The width of the curb ramp shall be a minimum dimension of 48 inches (1.2 meters) exclusive of flared sides or wings. On existing sidewalks only, where 48 inches (1.2 meters) is not feasible, a minimum width of 36 inches (0.9 meters), exclusive of flared sides or wings shall be allowed. If a curb ramp is located where pedestrians must walk across the ramp, or where it is not protected by handrails or guardrails, it shall have flared sides. Curb ramps with returned curbs may be used where pedestrians would not normally walk across the ramp.

Height Requirements

Height of the railing is particularly important for decks that sit higher off the ground. If the deck is 30" or more above the ground or next level then a guardrail is required on all open sides. Guardrails must be a minimum of 36" high from the surface. If there is adjacent, fixed seating against the edge the guardrails must be at least 36" higher than the seating.

Additionally, you can't have a gap wider than 4" between the surface of the deck and the bottom of the railing.

Strength Requirements

Your deck railing will understandably undergo a lot of pressure. According to the building codes, guardrails must have adequate strength to support minimum loads. The requirements laid out in the IBC states that the guardrail must be able to handle a load of 50 lbs. per linear foot.

Anchoring Requirements

Anchoring is an important aspect of the safety of the railing. Guardrails will be deemed unsafe if they aren't properly anchored or if the components used to anchor the railing can't support the nominal load limits. In addition, the railing should be anchored within 36" of the edge of the open sides.

R311.2.1 Guards required. Porches, balconies or raised floor surfaces located more than 30" above the floor or grade below shall have guards not less than 36" in height. Open sides of stairs with a total rise of more than 30" above the floor or grade below shall have guards not less than 34" in height measured vertically from the nosing of the treads. Porches and decks which are enclosed with insect screening shall be equipped with guards where the walking surface is located more than 30" above the floor or grade below.

R311.2.2 Under stair protection. Enclosed accessible space under stairs shall have walls, under stair surface, and any soffits protected on the enclosed side with 1/2" gypsum board.

R311.5.2 Headroom. The minimum headroom in all parts of the stairway shall not be less than 6' 8" measured vertically from the sloped plane adjoining the tread nosing or from the floor surface of the landing or platform.

R311.5.3 Treads & Risers. The maximum riser height shall be 7 3/4" and the minimum tread depth shall be 10". The riser height shall be measured vertically between leading edges of the adjacent treads. The tread depth shall be measured horizontally between the vertical planes of the foremost projection of adjacent treads and at a right angle to the tread's leading edge. The walking surface of treads and landings of a stairway shall be sloped no steeper than one unit vertical in 48 units horizontal (2% slope). The greatest riser height within any flight of stairs shall not exceed the smallest by more than 3/8". The greatest tread depth within any flight of stairs shall not exceed the smallest by more than 3/8".

R311.5.3.2 Winders. Winders are permitted, provided that the width of the tread at a point not more than 12" from the side where the treads are narrower is not less than 10" and the minimum width of any tread is not less than 6".

R311.5.3.3 Profile. Open risers are permitted, provided that the opening between treads does not permit the passage of a 4" diameter sphere.

Exception: The opening between adjacent treads is not limited on stairs with a total rise of 30" or less.

R311.5.6 Handrails. Handrails shall be provided on at least one side of each continuous run of treads or flight with 4 or more risers.

R311.5.6.1 Height. Handrails for stairways shall be continuous for the full length of the flight, from a point directly above the top riser of the flight to a point directly above the lowest riser of the flight.

R311.5.6.2. Continuity. Handrails for stairways shall be continuous for the full length of the flight, from a point directly above the top riser of the flight to a point directly above the lowest riser of the flight. Handrails shall be returned or shall terminate in newel posts or safety terminals. Handrails adjacent to a wall shall have a space of not less than 1.5" between the wall and the handrails.

Exceptions: 1) Handrail shall be permitted to be interrupted by a newel post at a turn. 2) The use of a volute, turnout, starting easing or starting newel shall be allowed over the lowest tread.

R311.5.6.3. Handrail grip size. All required handrails shall be one of the following types or provide equivalent graspability.

> **1. Type I.** Handrails with a circular cross section shall have an outside diameter of at least 1 1/2 " and not greater than 2". If the handrail is not circular, it shall have a perimeter dimension of at least 4" and not greater than 6 1/4" with a maximum cross section dimension of 2 1/4'.
>
> **2. Type II.** Handrails with a perimeter greater than 6 1/4" shall provide a graspable finger recess area on both sides of the profile. The finger recess shall begin within a distance of 1/4" measured vertically from the tallest portion of the profile and achieve a depth at least 5/16" within 7/8" below the widest of the profile. This required depth shall continue for at least 3/8' to a level that is not less than 1 3/4" below the tallest portion of the profile. The minimum width of the handrail above the recess shall be 1 1/4" to a maximum of 2 3/4".

R311.5.8.1 Spiral stairs. Spiral stairways are permitted, provided the minimum width shall be 26" with each tread having a 7½" minimum tread width at 12" from the narrow edge. All treads shall be identical, and the rise shall be no more than 9½". A minimum headroom of 6' 6" shall be provided.

R312.2 Guard opening limitations. Required guards on open sides of stairways, raised floor areas, balconies, and porches shall have intermediate rails or ornamental closures that do not allow passage of a sphere 4" (102 mm) or more in diameter.

> **Exceptions:** 1) The triangular openings formed by the riser, tread and bottom rail of a guard at the open side of a stairway are permitted to be of such a size that a sphere 6 inches (152 mm) cannot pass through.
>
> 2) Openings for required guards on the sides of stair treads shall not allow a sphere 4-3/8 inches (107 mm) to pass through.

R314.1 Width. Stairways shall not be less than 36" in clear width at all points above the permitted handrail height and below the required headroom height. Handrails shall not project more than 4.5" on either side of the stairway and the minimum clear width of the stairway at and below the handrail height, including treads and landings, shall not be less than 31.5" where a handrail is installed on one side and 27" where handrails are provided on both sides.

> **Exception:** The width of spiral stairways shall be in accordance with Section R314.5.

R314.6 Circular stairways. Circular stairways shall have a tread depth at a point not more than 12" from the side where the treads are narrower of not less than 10" and the minimum depth of any tread shall not be less than 6". Tread depth at any walking line measured a consistent distance from a side of the stairway shall be uniform as specified in.

Landings at doors. The exterior landing at an exterior doorway shall not be more than 7 ¾ inches below the top of the threshold, provided the door, other than an exterior storm or screen door does not swing over the landing. There is no minimum height of landing in the code.

Stairways. Stairways shall not be less than 36 inches in clear width at all points above the permitted handrail height. It shall not project more than 4.5 inches on either side of the stairway. It shall not be less than 31.5 inches where a handrail is installed on one side and 27 inches where handrails are provided on both sides.

Stair treads and risers. The maximum riser height shall be 7 ¾ inches. The minimum tread depth shall be 10 inches. The tread depth shall be measured horizontally between the vertical planes of the adjacent treads and at a right angle to the tread's leading edge. Handrails shall be provided on at least one side of each continuous run of treads or flight of stairs with four or more risers. Handrail height shall not be less than 34 inches and not more than 38 inches. The use of a volute, turnout, starting easing or starting newel shall be allowed over the lowest tread.

Guards. Porches, balconies, ramps or raised floor surfaces located more than 30 inches above the floor or grade below shall have guards not less than 36 inches. Porches and decks which are enclosed with insect screening shall be equipped with guards. Guard opening limitations. Openings for required guards on the sides of stair treads shall not allow a sphere 4 3/8 inch to pass through.

Deck stairway. Decks need to be designed for 40 psf live load, plus the dead load of the building material. Individual stair treads shall be designed for the uniformly distributed live load or a 300 pound concentrated load acting over an area of 4 square inches, whichever produces the greater stresses.

Landings at stairways. There shall be a floor or landing at the top and bottom of each stairway. The width of each landing shall not be less than the width of stairway served. Every landing shall have a minimum dimension of 36 inches measured in the direction of trave.

Landings at stairways. A floor or landing is not required at the top of an interior flight of stairs, including stairs in an enclosed garage, provided a door does not swing over the stairs.

Winder treads shall have a minimum tread depth of 10 inches measured at a point 12 inches from the side where the treads are narrower. Winder treads shall have a minimum tread depth of 6 inches at any point. Minimum width shall be 26 inches with each tread having a 7 1/2 inches minimum tread depth at 12 inches from the narrower edge. All treads shall be identical, and the rise shall be no more than 9 1/2 inches. A minimum headroom of 6 feet 6 inches shall be provided. Spiral stairways. All treads shall be identical, and the rise shall be no more than 9 1/2 inches. A minimum headroom of 6 feet 6 inches shall be provided.

References

IPMC – International Property Maintenance Code

IRC – International Residential Code

www.ingramcontent.com/pod-product-compliance
Lightning Source LLC
Chambersburg PA
CBHW071405160426
42813CB00084B/469